TABLE OF CONTENTS

What makes this guide unique? -------------------------------1

Introduction--4

What is investing? --8

Benefits --12

Define your goals---21

Find the perfect time to start --------------------------------26

Financing a real estate property ----------------------------35

Finding the first investment property -----------------------50

Analyzing the property---59

Building a team --80

Should I Start an LLC? --88

Common pitfalls---93

Controversial American Dream ----------------------------105

Final Words ---119

Bonus Content ---123

What Makes This Guide Unique?

Perfect for beginners!

This guide is perfect if you are getting started in real estate investing. You know you want to invest but don't know how to start. This guide has all the answers for you.

Free Bonus Content!

The bonus content included is extremely valuable. The value of the guide goes beyond the chapters included. You will also receive actual templates to analyze the properties.

Free Updates!

We will send you updates to the guide anytime we make them. We will also make available to you any new property analysis tools as soon as they become available.

Just make sure to join the newsletter by scanning the QR code at the end of this book so that we know where to notify you of any updates or new related books published.

Ready to Get Started?

The great thing about investing in real estate is that success depends largely on the actions you take. There is no employer or boss to have to deal with. You are in total control of how successful you become. If you shelf this guide and do nothing with the information learned, you won't achieve anything. If you decide to learn more and take action, you would be surprised by what you could accomplish.

Now it is completely and utterly up to you, *and no one by you*, where you take it from here.

When will you start taking control of your financial future?

CHAPTER 1

Introduction

I'm writing this guide to real estate investing to help wanna-be real estate investors **get started**. This short-read is perfect for individuals interested but hesitant to **take the first step**.

Most wanna-be real estate investors have heard about the subject of real estate investment. Many are interested in buying and renting properties. Others often think about buying, fixing then selling properties. This guide focuses largely on the aspect of **buying and renting properties**.

There are no secrets to real estate investing. There is just knowledge to be gained over time.

In this guide we go over the different aspects of investing in general. Then we describe what investing in real estate can do for you. We go over defining goals and finding the perfect time to start.

Then we focus further on how to find a real estate rental property, analyze it thoroughly and secure financing for it.

- What does it mean to invest in real estate?
- What benefits are there to be gained?
- How do you go about starting?
- Who do you need to talk to?
- Should you start an LLC?
- Are you afraid of making mistakes?

Keep on reading to find answers to questions or concerns that may be preventing you from taking the first step, moving forward and buying your first real estate rental investment property.

This guide cuts to the chase and is not long-winded with stories and a bunch of motivational fluff.

This is simply a guide of how a beginner can start investing in real estate.

CHAPTER 2

What Is Investing?

In a nutshell, investing is using money to make money.

Investing is:

- Making money grow
- Putting your money to work for you
- Growing your net worth
- Being disciplined
- Thinking long term
- Taking control of your finances

Investing is NOT necessarily:

- Getting rich quick
- Quitting your job tomorrow
- Letting others manage your money

Investment Types

While this ebook is focused on Real Estate Investing, it is important to highlight a few other basic investment types in order to put things in context.

Now more than ever, there are many ways to invest your money. In today's complex financial world, there are numerous investment vehicles to choose from.

Many of these investment types can help you achieve your financial goals of growing your money and potentially retiring early:

Bank products: Savings accounts and CDs earn interest. In 2015, the annual average interest rate in savings account was 1.4%. In 2016, the highest I could find by shopping online was 1.2%. That's barely enough to keep up with inflation. Savings accounts are good to set money aside in for emergencies and short-term savings for events that require quick access to cash.

Stocks: Stock trading is buying shares of a company's stock. Stocks come in a large variety and are often described based on the company type, size and performance. Investing in stocks can have short-term and long-term growth.

Bonds: Investing in bonds means that you, the investor, loan money to an organization in exchange for interest payments. When you buy a bond, you are lending to the bond issuer that may be a government municipality, or corporation.

Funds: Funds are typically mutual funds or exchange-traded funds (ETFs). The funds pool money from many investors and invest it according to a specific investment strategy. An ETF hold assets such as stocks, commodities, or bonds, and trades close to its net asset value over the course of the trading day. You can select funds that offer diversification that meets your needs and risk tolerance. Reading the prospectus of a fund is important to learn the intricate details of the fund.

Other investment types include annuities, college saving (529), retirement (401K), options, commodity futures, security futures, insurance products, and various alternative and complex products.

So What?

I am all for diversification and against putting all your money in one asset class such as the stock market or real estate alone.

I am by no means a financial expert and you should definitely seek advice from a financial advisor. In separate ebooks, I will emphasize the importance of getting involved in the stock market and investing for long term growth.

With that said, my personal preference remains real estate. Keep on reading to find out what real estate investing can do for you.

CHAPTER 3

Benefits

In a nutshell, investing in real estate builds wealth.

Here are 7 benefits of real estate investment:

- Cash flow from rental income
- Appreciation
- Principal paydown
- Inflation hedge
- Tax benefits
- Debt leverage
- Equity leverage

Investing in real estate is NOT necessarily:

- Making money without doing any work at all.

- Letting others totally manage your properties without any oversight from you.
- Risk free.

Cash Flow from Rental Income

Cash flow from rental income is the money you make renting the property.

For example, if the tenant pays $1500 and all expenses amount to $1000, then you are cash flowing $500.

Cash flow is the amount of money you end up with after collecting rent and paying all expenses such as the mortgage payment and maintenance costs. It is basically your profit, also known as Net Operating Income (NOI). I will cover methods of calculating NOI in following chapters.

Appreciation

Appreciation is the increase in the property's value over time.

Real estate has proven to be an excellent source of profit. It is not possible though to predict real estate trends that vary significantly due to economic conditions. However, over the long term, real estate seems to always appreciate and go up in value. The "great recession" that started in December of 2007 brought the global financial system in its knees and lasted 18 months. The recession was caused largely by the US subprime mortgage crisis. So the impact on housing was severe. Home prices plummeted. By the end of the 2016, on average, home prices have recovered nearly all losses (before adjusting for inflation).

This goes to prove that investing in real estate is inherently risky. But if your investment strategy is focused on slow and steady growth while cash flowing from rental income, then you shouldn't lose any sleep during economic downturns.

Here is a house price index graph from The Economist showing American house prices since 1980.

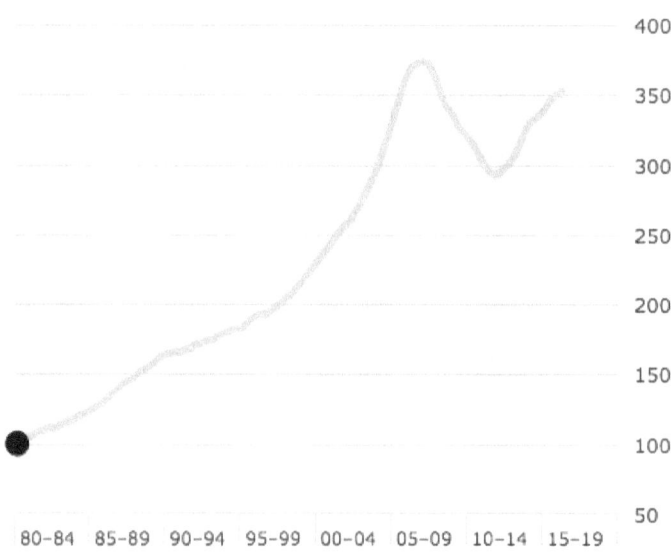

Source:

http://www.economist.com/blogs/graphicdetail/2016/08/daily-chart-20

Principal Paydown

Principal paydown is the reduction of the mortgage principal.

The mortgage principal is the outstanding balance of the mortgage. Every monthly mortgage payment reduces the mortgage principal. In effect, this is the act of principal paydown.

When you own a rental property, the tenant is indirectly chipping away at the principal and ultimately getting rid of the mortgage for you so that you could own it free and clear.

Inflation Hedge

Inflation hedge is investing in assets that provide protection against the decreased value of currency. Typically, assets such as gold and real estate are a great inflation hedge.

To the contrary, investing in stocks is not necessarily inflation proof. For example, if you invest your money in the stock market and average a 4% return, but inflation is 5%, you are losing money or buying power.

Investing in real estate rental properties tends to offer protection against inflation because the real estate returns are linked to the rental income received from tenants.

Almost always, real estate cash flow tends to increase over time such as at the end of the lease term or when a new tenant moves in.

Your mortgage payment remains the same but rental income increases over time. This results in a slow and steady increase of the cash flow.

Tax Benefits

The primary tax benefits of investing in real estate are deductions and depreciation.

You can deduct the rental expenses from rental income you earn. This reduces your tax liability. A lot of rental property expenses can be deducted in the year you spend the money.

For example, you can deduct regular maintenance, repair, home office expenses, professional services, legal services, bookkeeping, accounting fees, attorney fees, marketing, advertising, business travel expenses, property taxes, mortgage insurance and more.

Depreciation is deducting the costs of buying and improving the rental property. This includes allowances for exhaustion, wear and tear of the property. You begin to depreciate your rental property when you place it in service.

For example, say you buy a house for $100,000 in December and rent it out on January 1st. When you file your tax return for that year, as long as the property was in service for the entire year, you can deduct $3636.36. You arrive at this number by taking the basis of $100,000 and dividing it by the IRS allowed 27.5 years.

$100,000 / 27.5 = $3636.36.

Debt Leverage

Debt leverage is the use of other people's money to increase the purchasing power and ultimately the return on your investment.

For example, say you have $100,000 set aside that you want to invest in real estate. Without debt leverage, the $100,000 can buy you, with all cash, one property worth $100,000.

To take advantage of debt leverage, you could put only $20,000 of your own money as a 20% down payment and borrow the rest in the form of a mortgage. The cash-on-cash return in this case will be significantly higher because you will be generating income on the property by investing only $20,000 of your money.

Continuing in the same example, that $100,000 that you had saved up can buy you a total of five properties if we follow the same financing method of $20,000 down per property and financing the rest.

$100,000 / $20,000 = 5 properties.

This is a perfect example of leveraging debt to own five properties with a combined value of $500,000 by investing only $100,000 of your money.

Without debt leverage, $100,000 can buy one $100,000 property. With debt leverage, $100,000 can buy five $100,000 properties. **This is 5 times the purchasing power and 5 times the rental cash flow.**

Equity Leverage

Equity is the difference between the fair market value of the property and the amount owed on the mortgage.

For example, if the value of the property is $100,000 and you owe the bank $80,000, then your equity is $20,000.

When you put 20% down, you automatically have 20% equity in the property. But as you pay down the mortgage, the equity gradually increases. It can be advantageous to take out equity loans to make improvements to the property or to engage in other real estate investment opportunities.

So What?

These are all examples of **your money making money**, borrowed money making money and wealth preservation by taking advantage of leverage, hedge and tax benefits.

If done right and prudently, investing in real estate can be lucrative. Now that you are familiar with the benefits of real estate investing, it's time to define your goals and preferred investment strategy to get started.

CHAPTER 4

Define Your Goals

In a nutshell, defining your goals is deciding what investment strategy you prefer and putting an action plan together to get started.

Questions that you should answer:

- Do you want to quit your job now? (hint: don't)
- Do you want to buy and rent properties?
- Do you want to flip houses?
- What is your risk tolerance?

Can you quit your job right now?

No. Period. That's it. End of sentence!

But in the interest of leaving no stones unturned, it is of paramount importance to understand the importance of debt leverage. I've covered leverage in the previous chapter.

To be clear, when starting from scratch with no significant wealth or assets to rely on, you need your job to help fund your investments. The bank will be looking at your job's income before approving your for a mortgage. Mortgages on investment properties are inherently riskier in the eyes of banks. The bank will look at your debt-to-income ratio (I will cover DTI in the financing chapter) when qualifying you for the mortgage given that the property is residential. You need to prove to the bank that you can afford making the mortgage payments even if the property is totally vacant and generating no money.

While this is largely the case for residential loans, it is not necessarily the case for loans for commercial properties. Banks typically have a dedicated department dealing with commercial loans.

Do you want to rent or flip properties or both?

In order to decide whether your strategy should be focused on renting or flipping properties, it's important to make a distinction between active income and passive income.

Passive income is earned with minimal effort on your part. Irrespective of where you decide to live, work or vacation, money keeps flowing into your bank account.

Active income, in contrast, requires you to be considerably more involved.

Renting

Renting properties can be largely passive in the sense that you don't necessarily have to be involved on a daily basis unless you're managing the property yourself. We will discuss operating the business later in this ebook.

Flipping

Flipping properties is very much considered active. You have to actively be involved in sourcing, buying, improving, marketing and ultimately selling the properties.

Start with the end in sight

To a certain degree, it is important to think long term and start investing in real estate with the end in sight. Where do you want to be 10 or 20 years down the road? Are you focused on increasing your net worth or are you solely working towards establishing sources of passive income to replace your salary? It is very helpful to define a set of guidelines that you could use to define your investment strategy.

So What?

First and foremost, again, don't quit your job yet. Remember that leverage is so important. And don't forget that your W2 job income is the biggest leverage you have when getting started.

Think big and create a long-term plan that allows you to achieve your real estate objectives.

While thinking big is critical, don't let planning stifle your ability to act.

Don't fall trap to analysis paralysis.

CHAPTER 5

Find the Perfect Time To Start

The perfect time to start is NOW. There is never a better time to start investing than NOW.

Procrastination is your worst enemy. Investing as early as possible in your life is the single most important thing to keep in mind when you are overthinking "timing".

The single question that you should answer:

Why have you not started investing in real estate yet?

Why have you not started investing in real estate yet?

- Lack of knowledge?
- Short on cash?
- Unable to find affordable properties?
- Scared of making a mistake?

Whatever your excuse is, it isn't big enough to prevent you from reaching your goals. Every problem has a solution. Instead of wasting your time thinking about why you have not started, divert your energy to learning the basics of getting started. Make a plan with small baby steps. Then, act! Buy your first property and adjust your plan as you go.

Timing the market

Timing the market is a game for losers and those who want to lose sleep worrying about when to buy and sell. This applies to the stock market and to some degree to real estate investing as well. Investing in real estate is a long-term play. Buying real estate when prices are low is obviously better than buying in a hot market. But this does not mean that you cannot act at all in a hot market. There are always lucrative opportunities that can be found in any market but only if you work hard to find them.

Learning is a journey

Focus on learning about real estate investing. Read books. Talk to friends who are investing. Join a club. Attend a seminar if you like but don't get ripped off at them signing up for things you don't need.

Learning is critical. But it is important to recognize that learning is a journey not a destination.

You will never know everything. So remember that your focus when getting started should be on learning the basics and not on learning everything under the sun. Get familiar with the important techniques of analyzing properties. Learn the ins and outs of real estate financing. Find a property. Buy it. Rent it. Then regroup and make the necessary tweaks to your plan. Rinse and repeat.

No money no honey

Short on cash? Fine. Let's start by agreeing that it is totally true that buying a real estate property without no money down is hard. However, you could buy a property with no money (or little money) down. We will cover financing options in the financing chapter. But let's set that aside for a moment. For the purpose of planning, it is ultra critical to make sure that your financial house is in order.

Get your financial house in order

If you are broke or living paycheck to paycheck, real estate investing should not be your focus, at least not yet. Jumping into real estate investing while your finances are a mess is reckless.

The cash that might be required for real estate investing goes beyond the potential down payment that might be needed. You need to think about other costs such as closing costs, rehab expenses if necessary, unexpected repairs and vacancies.

The lack of cash should not lead you to abandon your real estate investing goals. But it is important to be prudent and realistic and not assume that investing in real estate will fix your financial problems and magically put cash in your pocket.

If your savings account is empty, work harder on replenishing it. Cut down unnecessary expenses and redirect some of your income to your savings account every month. Get a part time job if necessary and save all the extra income. Many of these things can be uncomfortable if you are not earning enough in the first place. Consider asking for a raise or getting another job that pays a little more.

If you are really motivated and truly care about investing in real estate, you will find a way to save money.

If you can't manage to save any money at all, real estate investing is not for you.

Getting your financial house in order is definitely a prerequisite before diving into real estate investing.

Affordable Properties

Finding affordable real estate properties is not hard but it can be somewhat frustrating in a hot real estate market.

If you live in San Francisco, New York or Washington DC, you could be looking at two-bedroom condos selling for half a million. Let us be clear that such properties are not what you should be looking at when starting the journey of real estate investing.

It may be discouraging when you start searching for properties in a hot market and not finding anything that makes financial sense. This is normal. A 20% down payment that may be needed for a $500,000 property is $100,000. The rental income barely pays the mortgage. Add the expected and unexpected operating expenses and you could be looking at a net loss of a few hundred dollars a month.

Shortly put, investing in hot markets and overpriced metropolitan areas is not for everyone. Certainly, it is not for those getting their feet wet in real estate investing. It is best to start exploring affordable areas and searching for much more affordable properties. There are hundreds of cities across the country with stable and affordable real estate markets. Several of these markets have numerous properties on the market for $75,000 - $200,000.

We will cover more on the topic of finding properties in the How to Find Your First Property chapter.

Scared of making a mistake

I have news for you. You will make mistakes! Put that fear of making mistakes behind you once for all.

Do your best and never seek to be perfect. Remember that perfectionism is your enemy. Perfectionism and analysis paralysis are best buddies.

Learn the basics. Make calculated informed decisions. Invest in a property that is well within your means. Don't take huge risks. Seek help. Ask a lot of questions. By investing prudently, you will reduce the chance of failure. And if you do fail in your first investment, it will be less likely to ruin you. You will be able to recover from the failure.

The only way to not make mistakes is to do nothing. And to do nothing is the biggest mistake.

So What?

Don't waste too much energy trying to find the best time to start. Just do it. Create a plan and work on executing it without reexamining it every day. If it is of any help at all, remember that you are not the first and won't be the last one to invest in real estate. It has been done before. Plenty of help is available. All you need to do is learning the basics, getting your financial house in order and taking the first step of buying your first investment property.

CHAPTER 6

Financing a Real Estate Property

Financing a real estate property requires decent understanding of the financing options available. Knowing your finances, understanding and maintaining a good credit history should be a priority especially if you are new to real estate investing.

Know your finances

Before embarking on the journey of real estate investing, knowing your finances is necessary in order to avoid mistakes. You need to know how much financial risk you can afford to take. You need to know how much you can afford to borrow without biting more than you could chew.

How much money can you allocate to real estate investing?

Determine how much money you can allocate in the form of a down payment to finance your first investment property.

If you have $50,000 saved up, you should be looking at a property to invest in with a purchase price of around $200,000. A 20% down payment on a $200,000 property is $40,000. This leaves you with $10,000 to spend on closing costs and other property improvement expenses that might be needed to prepare the property for rent.

Better yet, if you have $50,000 saved up, you could consider buying two properties instead of one. $50,000 / 2 = $25,000 as a down payment on each property with a sale price of $100,000 each. This leaves you with $5,000 of cash per property.

These are just basic examples that should help you remain realistic while assessing your financial ability to invest in real estate using conventional financing.

How good are your credit history and credit score?

Having a clean credit history as well as good credit score is extremely helpful in receiving financing for your investment property.

This is particularly true for new investors, which is what we're focused on in this book. Your goal when financing your first real estate investment property should be receiving low interest financing from a reputable lender.

> *Having good credit is the cornerstone of affordable low interest financing.*

If you are putting 20% down on a $200,000 property and financing the rest $160,000, your monthly mortgage payment (including an estimated $258 in taxes and insurance) will be $1,022. The assumption is that your credit is great which qualifies you for an interest rate of 4% on a 30-year fixed-rate mortgage.

Following the same assumptions, here is how the numbers deteriorate to your disadvantage if you credit is less than favorable which drives the interest rate higher:

Mortgage amount	Mortgage term in years	Credit Score	Interest	Mortgage Payment
$160,000	30	780+	4%	$1,022
$160,000	30	680-699	4.250%	$1,045
$160,000	30	620-639	4.625%	$1,080
$160,000	30	< 620	Good Luck!	

You can replicate the same results by using online calculators from your favorite lenders.

A credit score lower than 620 puts you at a major disadvantage when attempting to secure financing for an investment property. Many lenders will not even approve you for a mortgage. Others will approve you but may require a bigger down payment and a higher interest rate.

Keep in mind that the examples depicted above are very basic and don't even take into consideration the details of your credit report itself. Beyond the score, the lender will review the details on your credit report. Your credit report includes information about your credit card accounts, student loans, personal loans and car loans. Your report will also show any late payments, collections, short sales, foreclosures and bankruptcies.

> *Anything negative on your credit report is likely to impact your credit score and subsequently the mortgage interest rate.*

There are several simple ways to get free credit reports:

- Free report per bureau once a year –
    - annualcreditreport.com
- Credit Karma – Free unlimited reports but full of ads to credit cards, etc..

- o creditkarma.com
- Your bank or credit card company –
    - o Log in to the online portal of your bank or credit card company and it is almost guaranteed that they offer free credit reports simply because you are their customer.

Know your debt-to-income ratio!

What is debt-to-income ratio?

Your debt-to-income ratio (or DTI) is the total of the monthly debt payments divided by your gross monthly income. To calculate your debt-to-income ratio, you add up all your monthly debt payments and divide them by your gross monthly income.

For example, if you have a car payment, student loan payment, several credit card payments and working on getting approved for a mortgage, you can add all these payments up to come up with your total monthly debt.

If your total monthly debt is $2,000 and your gross monthly income is $6,000, then your debt-to-income ratio is $2,000 / $6,000 = 0.33 or 33%.

Monthly Gross Income	Monthly Debt Payments
$6,000	
	$400 car payment
	$150 student loan
	$20 credit card minimum payment
	$50 credit card minimum payment
	$1,380 mortgage payment
Total Income	Total Debt
$6,000	$2,000
% Debt-to-income ratio = $2,000 / $6,000 = 33%	

Why is debt-to-income ratio important?

This ratio is an important number that lenders look at when assessing your ability to make the mortgage payments.

Studies suggest that borrowers with a higher debt-to-income ratio are more likely to run into trouble making monthly payments. For that reason, most lenders avoid lending to borrowers with 43 percent or higher debt-to-income ratio.

As with everything, there are some exceptions and variations. The 43 percent ratio is not always set in stone and does vary higher or lower based on the risk appetite of each lender. Some lenders might accept a 44 or 45 percent debt-to-income ratio if they are convinced that you will be able to make the mortgage payments.

Mortgage Types

There are several types of mortgages to choose from. You can discuss them with your lender to see which one makes the most sense to you based on your financial situation.

Fixed-rate loan or adjustable-rate mortgage

When deciding on the type of loan, first you need to determine if a fixed-rate loan or an adjustable-rate loan is right for you.

Fixed-rate mortgages

By far, the most preferred mortgages are fixed-rate. The interest rate is fixed. This means that it remains unchanged throughout the term of the 10 to 30 year mortgage. The most common terms are 15 and 30 years. Either way, the interest remains the same.

The benefit of fixed-rate mortgages is the security they offer the borrower. You will not have to worry about increases in the interest rate that will increase the monthly mortgage payment.

A shorter-term mortgage like 10 or 15 years will always have a lower interest than longer-term mortgages like 20 or 30 years.

Adjustable-rate mortgages (ARMs)

Adjustable-rate mortgages always offer lower interest rates than fixed-rate mortgages, at least at first. Then the interest rate will start fluctuating. The time of when the interest will change depends on the adjustment interval of the mortgage you choose.

For example:

- A 30-year 3/1 ARM will have a fixed interest rate for 3 years then the rate will change every year for 27 years.
- A 30-year 5/1 ARM will have a fixed interest rate for 5 years then the rate will change every year for 25 years.

- A 30-year 7/1 ARM will have a fixed interest rate for 7 years then the rate will change every year for 23 years.

- A 30-year 10/1 ARM will have a fixed interest rate for 3 years then the rate will change every year for 20 years.

The benefit of adjustable-rate mortgages is the up-front initial low interest rate, which means lower mortgage payments for the first years of the mortgage. But this doesn't automatically mean that ARMs are always better. You will have to think long term and determine if you will be keeping the property for a long time or not. If you are keeping the property for only 3 years then maybe a 3/1 ARM can be great for you.

But generally, adjustable-rate mortgage lack a level of comfort and security especially for long-term investments. What if you end up keeping the property longer than the initial fixed-rate period? Will you still be able to afford the mortgage payments? Will your property still be profitable and generating enough cashflow?

Other mortgages and methods of financing

Since we're focused here on getting started in real estate investing, we will keep the financing chapter focused on the basics of getting started. But we will go over other financing options briefly.

Non-conventional mortgages

Conventional mortgages are mortgages not backed by the government. On the other hand, non-conventional mortgages are mortgages backed by the government. They include Federal Housing Administration (FHA) loans, Veterans Administration (VA) loans, and US Department of Agriculture (USDA) loans.

Federal Housing Administration (FHA) loans

FHA loans are mortgages insured by the Federal Housing Administration. They are intended for borrowers who are unable to secure a large down payment or have less than adequate credit.

FHA loans allow for down payments as low as 3.5 percent. These are generally popular for first-time homeowners and very much unlikely to be used by real estate investors investing in multiple rental properties. With that said, a low down payment of 3.5 percent might be your only avenue of getting started if this is your first purchase and you are low on cash. You can live in the property and refinance later, move out, rent it out and move on to purchase more properties.

Veterans Administration (VA) loans

VA loans allow for zero money down for qualifying borrowers such as active military, military families and veterans. If you qualify for a VA loan, it makes perfect sense to get one. You will never have to pay any mortgage insurance and the Veterans Administration guarantees the loan for the lender.

USDA loans

The US Department of Agriculture loans are designed to buy and renovate homes in rural areas for the most part. USDA loans are known for their low interest rates and no money down.

Jumbo loans

Jumbo loans are loans that do not conform to the landing guidelines of Fannie Mae and Freddie Mac.

Fannie Mae and Freddie Mac are government-sponsored enterprises. They are privately owned and receive support from the government. Their primary function is that they purchase conforming mortgages from the lenders who originate them.

A conforming (non-jumbo) loan is a home loan that adheres to the landing guidelines of Fannie Mae and Freddie Mac. The guidelines include specific requirements for income and creditworthiness that the borrower must meet. Another requirement is the loan amount limit. The limit varies by the market location you're purchasing the property in.

For example, in 2017 the loan amount limit that would conform to the guidelines is $424,100 in most counties. But in high-cost areas, the limit increases accordingly. In San Francisco, it is $636,150.

A Jumbo loan is a loan that does not meet the requirements of Fannie Mae and Freddie Mac.

So what?

Now that you know the basic characteristics of the various mortgage types available, you should be better prepared to engage a lender and ask the right questions. Every situation varies so it's impossible to suggest one mortgage type over another. You will need to consult with a mortgage advisor you trust and possibly consult with an accountant if necessary to better understand your finances.

Also, it is important to remember what caused the financial crisis of 2008. In one word, it was greed! Jumbo loans, risky loans, predatory lending practices and buyers biting more than they could chew. It is important to learn from that financial disaster and proceed with caution.

It is easy to blame the banks and the government. But despite what banking institutions make available to us, it is important for us to not take the bait. Sure, zero down payment loans are available but it does not mean they are good for you.

For the purpose of real estate investing, our preference remains 30-year fixed-rate conventional mortgages with a 20% to 25% down payment. Keep reading to find out how to find attractive investment properties and how to analyze them to figure out the cash flow and return on your cash invested.

CHAPTER 7

Finding the First Investment Property

Finding your first investment property is very much similar to finding a personal property. The fact that you are aiming to invest in and possibly rent the property does not make the search process any different. The search criteria are certainly critical to ensure the property is profitable and worth investing in but the search process remains the same. Let's cover the different methods of looking and finding rental properties. In the next chapter, we will dive into the details of analyzing the properties from a financial perspective.

Where do I start looking for my first rental property?

The short answer is: Everywhere!

Being a new real estate investor, you need to be all eyes and ears and leave no stone unturned. This means that you need to talk to friends and family. You need to make it known that you are interested in real estate in general and in investment properties in particular. By doing just that, you give yourself a greater chance of finding investment opportunities.

Find rental property by networking

Networking should be at the heart of your real estate investment strategy. By networking with other investors, friends, family, investment clubs, friends of friends and real estate agents, you could potentially find rental properties before they are officially listed on the market.

Networking is the good old-fashioned word-of-mouth approach to doing business. Knowing someone, or someone who knows someone, still works.

If you know that a friend of yours has a cousin who invests in real estate, ask your friend to arrange for the three of you to meet for coffee to just discuss and compare your strategies. Most real estate investors don't mind meeting new investors. They can tell you about properties they have been investing in and you can tell them about your goals too. They can help point you in the right direction and share with you their experiences, which could help you avoid common pitfalls.

Find rental property online

Searching for your first investment rental property online is the most convenient way. From the convenience of your kitchen table or wherever you like to kill some time browsing social media and the corners of the internet, you can choose to do something much more useful by searching for properties.

Search for properties nearby or anywhere else in the country. Do this to get yourself more familiar with the real estate markets. We spend hours browsing the Internet aimlessly hopping from one site to another. Doing the same without much planning when looking for a real estate property is not too bad. The worst that can happen is that you will, at least, know more about property costs and rental rates in various markets.

You can use numerous websites to find real estate listings, such as:

Zillow.com

Realtor.com

Redfin.com

Trulia.com

All these online platforms generally yield the same search results from the Multiple Listing Service (MLS).

You can narrow the search down by selecting a location radius, property type, number of bedrooms, bathrooms, garages, age of property, square footage, and price.

If the property will be a rental, you can also add specific keywords to search for. For example, you could search for "duplex" or "rental". Adding such keywords limits your search results dramatically because it is not guaranteed that all listings will be detailed enough to include all the keywords that could be of interest to you.

Zillow.com for example makes it particularly easy to search for properties for sale and for rent at the same time. You can toggle between both views and search results to get a better understanding of the potential rental rates in the market you are interested in.

Also, virtually all sites give you the option to save your favorite search criteria and have the results emailed to your periodically. For example, you could save a search criteria for single-family homes with 3 bedrooms and 2 bathrooms, within 10 miles of downtown Cleveland, between $100,000 and $120,000 and have the results emailed to you daily.

When looking at properties online, most sites also display conveniently the sales history of each property and the taxes paid in previous years. This information is extremely essential to analyzing the real estate property, which we will cover later.

Find rental property through real estate agents

Real estate agents exist to help buyers buy houses and sellers sell houses. When you look at it this simplistically, you will see that finding investment rental properties through real estate agents makes perfect sense.

You can start by reaching out to the listing agent of the property you are interested in. The agent's contact information is typically included in the listing details online. Or you can reach out to any agent of your choosing, perhaps one recommended by a friend.

Don't shy away from divulging to the agent your plan of buying the property for investment. It is perfectly acceptable to ask the agent if the property would be suitable as a rental. You can also discuss the rental market in the area and rental rates for comparable properties.

Keep in mind that not all agents have the patience or the know-how to work with real estate investors. Many agents prefer working with personal homebuyers who aren't terribly concerned with the profitability of the property or the return on investment.

Personal homebuyers are typically focused on finding houses with an open concept great for entertaining guests, two-car garage and in a location of a great school district. A personal home criteria as such is the sweet spot for many agents. So if you notice that your agent is not being very helpful with discussing your interest in investment properties, you can ask the agent if there is another agent they could recommend who typically works with investors. It is also perfectly normal to ask the agent if they could recommend property managers in the area.

Find rental property through property managers

Property managers work for property management companies. You can hire them to manage your property from finding and managing the relationship with tenants to coordinating repairs and other services.

But beyond their primary scope of work and even before you hire them property managers can be a great source of information about the markets you are interested in. They can send your way investment opportunities that they come across.

Property managers usually know best whether a property is worth investing in as a rental. Simply getting in touch with one or two of them can add great value. Ask them how much the property could rent for. Ask them where they operate mainly and what properties and areas they are usually more successful in at keeping properties occupied.

Find rental property at auctions

Buying properties at auctions is typically not a common method for new and inexperienced investors. This is the case for several reasons. There is an inherent risk to buying properties at auctions in the first place. There is the unknown factor that can be intimidating for you if this is your very first investment property.

Auction.com is the most popular website for auctions. You can search for properties and see the opening bid for each property. The auction types you will find include short sales, foreclosures and post foreclosures (REOs) as well.

The auctions do take place online, at a designated location or at the courthouse. Buying a property at an auction requires a deposit that you must have on you in the form of a cashier's check. If you win the bid, you must return very shortly to pay for the property in full. Securing financing in advance is critical in this case. Given the high risk of buying properties at auctions, we will not cover them in this book since we're focused primarily on helping new investors buy their first investment property.

So what?

Searching for properties to invest in is relatively simple. Looking for properties for sale online is the easiest way to get your search going. But, networking and talking to people like friends, realtors and property managers is the most effective and valuable method to "get it right".

While searching and identifying properties that may be of interest to you seems very straightforward, and it is, the next logical step is analyzing the property from a financial perspective to determine if you should buy it. This is precisely where the rubber meets the road. Keep on reading!

CHAPTER 8

Analyzing the Property

What is "analyzing a rental property"?

The short answer is: Everything! Without analyzing a rental property, there is no way of knowing if the investment is even worth considering.

Analyzing a rental property is a process that varies from one investor to another. Some tend to do it on the fly; others tend to use spreadsheets religiously. While there may be several variables and factors involved in analyzing properties, one thing is always true, investors analyze properties to determine if they are worth investing in.

So, how do we analyze a prospective rental property?

We will calculate the mortgage, income, expenses and focus on target numbers and common practices to determine if a property is worth investing in.

Do not get overwhelmed by this process. It will get easier significantly when you leverage the bonus content and the template we provide.

Rental property Assumptions

In the calculations and examples we will outline, we will be assuming that financing will consist of a 20% down payment and a 30-year fixed rate mortgage at 4% interest. The property will cost $120,000. You can adjust and tweak your assumptions as needed in the excel template we provide in the bonus content.

Rental Property Mortgage

Down Payment

The property is on the market for $120,000. Let's assume that the sales price will be the full asking price.

Sales Price x 20% = Down Payment Amount

$120,000 x 20% = $24,000

Financed Amount (Mortgage Balance)

Since we're putting $24,000 down, let's figure out how much we need to finance.

Sales Price - Down Payment = Financed Amount

$120,000 - $24,000 = $96,000

Monthly Mortgage Debt Payment

The easiest way to calculate the monthly debt payment of the mortgage is by using the PMT formula in Excel or Google Sheets. The PMT formula helps us calculate the monthly debt payment, which includes the principal and interest. It does not include the property taxes and insurance part of the mortgage payment. We will add them later.

=PMT(4%/12,360,96000) = -$458.32

- 4% is the annual interest rate. We divide it by 12 is to convert it to monthly.
- 360 is the total number of months of the mortgage term. 30 years x 12 months = 360 months.
- 96000 is the financed amount after the 20% down payment on the $120,000 property.

When we type this formula exactly as is in Excel or Google Sheets,

=PMT(4%/12,360,96000)

We will get:

-$458.32

That's minus $458.32. It is expected for the number to be negative since it is the amount owed.

$458.32 is the monthly amount of Principal and Interest (PI).

Monthly Mortgage Taxes & Insurance

The taxes are easily found in the listing (on Zillow, Realtor, etc...) right in the listing typically under the property history/taxes section. Look for the amount of taxes paid in the last year on file.

The property insurance can be estimated. But we can get an even better estimate by contacting an insurance agent.

Let's assume that the annual property taxes will be $3,000 and property insurance $500.

The monthly mortgage Taxes & Insurance (TI) will be $3,500 per year.

$3,500 / 12 = $291.66 per month.

Total Monthly Mortgage Payment

The total monthly mortgage payment consists of the mortgage Principal + Interest + Taxes + Insurance (PITI). This is how much we will owe the bank every month. This is our total mortgage payment.

In our example, we will be looking at $458.32 for PI and $291.66 for TI.

$458.32 + $291.66 = $749.99

Rental Mortgage Summary

Sales Price	Down Payment	Financed Amount
$120,000	$24,000 (20%)	$96,000

Financed Amount	Mortgage Terms	Mortgage Payment (PITI)
$96,000	30-year fixed at 4% interest	$749.99

Rental property income

When you identify a property that you are interested in buying and renting, it is important to figure out how much you think you can rent it for. Determining the potential rental income is relatively easy and can be done by relying on current properties advertised for rent on Zillow and other websites. You can also inquire about the rent rates by asking real estate agents and property managers.

You could be looking at a single-family house in which case the income is likely to come from one single source with is the tenant or family renting the property. And if you are looking at a student rental property with 4 bedrooms rented separately, you could be looking at 4 separate sources of income, one from each student tenant.

Either way, let's assume that the total rental income will be $1,800 per month.

Based on your risk appetite, you can assume that the property will be rented yearlong or you can be more conservative and assume that you will have to deal with some vacancy. In this example, we will very conservative and assume that the property will be vacant for a full month each year.

$1800 per month x 11 months = $19,800 yearly rental income

Rental property expenses

Property Management

We will be hiring a property manager to manage the property from end-to-end. We will assume that the property management company will charge 10% of the monthly rent.

$1,800 monthly rent x 10% = $180 per month in property management fees

Repairs and Maintenance

Repairs and maintenance are the most difficult numbers to calculate and forecast for a rental property.

How do we factor in replacing a fridge, water heater, air conditioning or the roof on a house? These are the capital expenditures that we will spend.

> *It's not a matter of if we will spend money on such expenses; it's a matter of when.*

A conservative method to keep capital expenditures in mind when analyzing a rental property is to assume that everything will break and need to be replaced over a period of 10 years. We might go for 5 years without any major repairs. But then we might get hit with several large bills for roof repair and several appliances breaking. We don't want such expenditures to catch us off-guard. For that reason, we will factor them in from the beginning. The idea is that we should be setting the money aside anyways so that the money is also available in the business checking account.

Let's assume that the total repair and maintenance costs over 10 years will be around $15,000.

This amounts to $15,000 / 10 years = $1,500 per year or $125 per month.

Other Rental Property Expenses

Other expenses might include a home association fee. We will assume that there isn't any in this case.

Utilities can be paid by the owner or the tenant. Situations vary so you can add it or leave it out based on the property and the specific circumstances.

Rental Property Net Operating Income

Before we can calculate the Net Operating Income, we need to know the Operating Income and Operating Expenses.

The operating income is the total money we collect before we pay the mortgage and expenses. The operating income is $19,800.

($1800 per month x 11 months = $19,800 yearly rental income.)

The operating expenses include all forms of expenses excluding the debt part of the mortgage. This includes taxes, insurance, property management, repairs and maintenance, and any other expenses we foresee. The operating expenses in this example amount to $7,160

The Net Operating Income (NOI) is the Operating Income - Operating Expenses.

$19,800 - $7,160 = $12,640 per year or $1,053.33 per month

Wait! This doesn't mean that we will be pocketing that amount. The Net Operating Income does not take the mortgage into consideration. The NOI is a very important to know. One day, we will have the mortgage paid off and the net operating income will be our cash flow. But in this example, we have a mortgage to deal with before we can figure out the actual cash flow.

Rental Property Cash flow

The rental property cash flow is the actual cash that we will earn after everything is said and done.

Net Operating Income - Debt = Cash Flow

The Debt is the Principal & Interest part of the mortgage payment. We determined above that PI would be $458.32 monthly or $5,500 yearly.

$12,640 - $5,500 = $7,140 yearly or $595.01 monthly

$595.01 is the actual cash we will keep each month.

Rental Property Depreciation

The IRS allows rental properties placed in service after 1986 to be depreciated over 27.5 years which is the amount of time the IRS considers the fair useful life of a rental property.

To calculate the annual depreciation, we take the tax assessment of the building value and divide it by 27.5. If the tax assessment of the $120,000 property in this example consists of $40,000 for the land and $80,000 for the building, we calculate the annual depreciation by dividing $80,000 by 27.5 years.

$80,000 / 27.5 = $2,909

This number is particularly useful when analyzing a property in order to know how much of the income will be taxable at the end of the year when you do your taxes.

Rental Property Taxable Net Income

Annual Cash flow + Annual Principal Only Payments - Depreciation = Taxable Net Income

$7,140 + $1,660 - $2,909 = $5,891

Out of the $7,140 that we are pocketing annually, only $5,891 will be taxed.

Rental Property Income & Expenses Summary

Net Operating Income

Net Operating Income = Operating Income - Operating Expenses

Operating Income	Operating Expenses	Net Operating Income
$19,800	$7,160	$12,640

Cash Flow

Cash Flow = Net Operating Income - Debt

Net Operating Income	Operating Expenses	Cash flow
$12,640	$5,500	$7,140

Taxable Net Income

Taxable Net Income = Cash Flow + Principal Payments - Depreciation

Cash flow	Principal Payments	Depreciation	Taxable Net Income
$7,140	$1,660	$2,909	$5,891

Again, do not get overwhelmed by this process. It will get easier significantly when you leverage the bonus content and the template we provide.

Analyzing the rental property deal

Now that we got the income and expenses down to science, it is time to look at some simple calculations that could help determine if the rental property is worth investing in. In the calculations below, we will be using the actual numbers already calculated in the property example above.

As mentioned previously, all these calculations are available seamlessly in the excel template we provide in the bonus contents. You just need to provide the variables in the template. All the other calculations, ratios and targets are automatically calculated.

Annual Cash-on-Cash Return on Investment (ROI)

The cash-on-cash Return on Investment (ROI) is perhaps the most indicative measure of a successful real estate investment rental property. It is a powerful measure focused on showing the return on the cash invested to buy the rental property.

In the example above, we've spent $24,000 as a 20% down payment to buy the rental property for $120,000. So the out of pocket cash invested so far is $24,000.

But the cash invested goes beyond the down payment. It is likely that we will need more cash to cover the closing costs and other potential initial rehab and repair costs before we can rent the property. Let's set aside $5,000 to cover the cost of painting, installing new flooring and replacing a couple of appliances. Let's also assume that the closing costs will be $5,000.

With those figures added, now we're looking at $24,000 + $5,000 + $5,000 = $34,000 in total cash invested.

To calculate the cash-on-cash return on investment we need to divide the Yearly Cash Flow calculated above by the Total Cash Invested.

Yearly Cash Flow / Total Cash Invested = Cash-on-Cash ROI

$7,140 / $34,000 = 0.21

$7,140 / $34,000 x 100 = 21%

The cash-on-cash ROI is 21%. This means that the yearly return on the total $34,000 invested is 21%.

Monthly Cash Flow Target of 33%

When analyzing the rental property, a quick measure we can use is the cash flow target percentage. You can set your own goal here. For example, you can decide that you want your monthly cash flow to be at least 33% of the Net Operating Income.

Annual Net Operating Income / 12 x 33.33% = Monthly Cash Flow Target of 33%

$12,640 / 12 x 33.33% = $351.08

At a quick glance, now you can see that your monthly cash flow goal should be a minimum of $351.08. Adjust the target percentage to suit your cash flow objective.

Monthly Income Target of 1.45%

Another target measure that we can use when quickly analyzing a property is the monthly income target. For example, you can decide that you want your monthly income target to be at least 1.45% of the purchase price of the rental property.

Purchase Price x 1.45% = Monthly Income Target of 1.45%

$120,000 x 1.45% = $1,740

This is an extremely simple calculation that helps you determine the minimum amount in monthly rental income to seek for the rental property. When searching for properties, you can quickly multiply the purchase price by 1.45% (or any other ratio of your choosing) to determine the minimum rental income that suits your objectives.

Capitalization (CAP) Rate of 10%

The CAP rate or capitalization rate is the ratio of Net Operating Income to property asset value.

Net Operating Income / Purchase Price = CAP Rate

$12,640 / $120,000 = 0.1053

$12,640 / $120,000 x 100 = 10.53%

The CAP rate is particularly useful if we purchase the property for all cash. But even when we're not, it is good to know the CAP rate. A CAP rate greater than 10% is generally considered good. Adjust it to suit your needs.

Debt Service Coverage Ratio (DSCR) Target of 1.35

The DSCR ratio is the Debt Service Coverage Ratio, also known as Debt Coverage Ratio (DCR). It is the ratio of cash we have available to pay the debt on the property.

For example, if the monthly net operating income is $900 and the mortgage is $1,000 then the DSCR is equal to 0.9. This means that we are $100 short and won't be able to afford making the mortgage payments.

Monthly Net Operating Income / Monthly Mortgage Payment = DSCR Ratio

$ 1,053.33 / $ 749.99 = 1.404

This means that the monthly net operating income is 1.404 times the monthly mortgage. It is a good sign that there should be enough money left each month to afford making the mortgage payments.

You can adjust the target to meet your needs. But keep in mind that the DSCR that banks look at vary but generally hover around 1.15–1.35.

So what?

Analyzing a rental property is where the rubber meets the road. The calculations, ratios and targets take the guesswork and emotions out of analyzing a rental property.

The numbers don't lie. But it is important to remember that you are in control of the ratios and targets and that you can tweak them to meet your risk appetite and investment requirements.

As always, consider seeking professional help when making important financial decisions. The general guidance provided here is just for educational purposes and should not be used instead of professional financial advice. Buying your first real estate rental property is an important financial decision. Proceed carefully and make calculated decisions but never let analysis paralyze you from taking any action at all.

CHAPTER 9

Building a Team

What is "building a team"?

Building a team is establishing a network of people you can reach out to and work with in all aspects of real estate investing.

Building a team is simply all about knowing people who can help you in achieving your goals. In the traditional sense, you are collecting business cards and the contact information of several individuals who can play a key role in helping you invest in real estate.

> *Building a team is not something you complete in a day or two. It is a journey.*

Building a team is a continuous process that gets enriched every time you meet a realtor, accountant, contractor or anyone else who you can work with in any aspect of real estate investing.

Who should be part of your team?

Realtor

You need a realtor or several realtors in your network. Realtors help you buy and sell properties but also can be a great source of leads. Leads are properties already on the market or about to be listed that agents can tell you about in advance.

When you establish a good relationship with realtors and explain to them your financial goals, they are very much likely to reach out to you and let you know when properties are available that meet your goals.

Loan Officer

A loan officer works for a bank or lender. A loan officer is the person you speak with when you are seeking financing for a real estate investment.

When you identify a property that you are interested in, you can reach out to your favorite loan officers asking for financing. Having them part of your team and network in advance only facilitates the process and makes the experience less tedious.

Accountant

An accountant can help you make better decisions when managing your business finances. A competent accountant can act as your advisor on overall accounting matters including taxes.

Perhaps you don't need to hire an accountant yet. But getting to know one or two can make the process easier later when you desperately need accounting advice.

Attorney or Lawyer

Real estate lawyers can offer legal advice on any issues you might encounter as a real estate investor. Some problems you might encounter include disputes with tenants, evictions, issues with the homeowner's association, noise from neighbors, deed recording issues, or any mortgage complications.

Just like you might not need an accountant today, you certainly might not need to hire a lawyer either. But it is important to have the contact information of one or two reputable lawyers with expertise in real estate.

Insurance Agent

An insurance agent can help put together the right insurance policy for your real estate property. If you already have a relationship with an insurance company, you can continue working with them. You can simply contact your insurance agent to ask for quotes on insuring your rental property.

Beyond insuring the rental property, ask your agent about getting a general liability insurance for your Limited Liability Company (LLC) if you have one. Also consider discussing with your agent getting a Personal Catastrophe Liability (PCL) insurance policy. A PCL policy, also known as Umbrella Insurance, is an extra liability insurance that could help protect you from major claims or lawsuits above the limits of other insurance policies you have.

Property Manager

Property managers help manage your rental property. Managing a rental property can involve preparing the property for rent, marketing and advertising the property, finding tenants, screening tenants and running the background checks, drawing up leasing agreements, moving tenants in, collecting rent, managing planned maintenance and emergency repairs, moving tenants out and evicting tenants if necessary.

Some property managers also go the extra mile and offer to represent you in court if that becomes necessary.

From a financial perspective, property managers also provide accounting property management services which can include making payments on your behalf such as mortgage, insurance, HOA dues, etc. Accounting services should also include complete monthly and annual documentation of income and expenses.

The services offered by property managers vary significantly. Reach out to several property managers and ask them about the specific services they offer.

Property managers can also be a great source of real estate leads. Get in touch with several property managers even if you are not prepared to hire one yet.

Contractor

Contractors can include handymen, carpenters, subcontractors and general contractors. Having several of them in your network is essential especially if you are investing in properties that need work. Whether the property is a fixer-upper or in need of minor repair, you might need to hire a contractor or several contractors to do the work.

A handyman might be the perfect choice for smaller odd jobs that you need done quickly. On the other hand, if the scope of work is big, you might be looking at hiring a general contractor who in turn can subcontract subcontractors and manage the entire project for you.

Do your homework and get everything down in writing.

So what?

Building your network is largely a planning and preparation exercise. Adding people with varying skillsets to your network puts you in a better position to make better decisions and tackle any issues in the futures.

It is true that you might not need an attorney or accountant today but it doesn't mean that you can't benefit from connecting with them in advance. You might be investing in turnkey properties that require no work at the moment, but you can still benefit from having contractors in your network. A day will come when you need help fixing something that you cannot do yourself.

If you are a jack-of-all-trades, good for you! It is generally a good thing. But think about whether it is worth it for you to do everything yourself versus hiring specialists to handle it. Do you really understand the tax laws surrounding real estate investing? Will you always have ample time to manage all your real estate rentals all on your own?

> *Give the bread dough to the baker even if he eats half of it.*
> *-Unknown*

Give the job to a person who knows how to do it best even if it will cost you. Think whether it makes financial sense to handle all aspects of real estate investment on your own or if you would be better off focusing your time and energy on investing in more properties and expanding your business.

Either way, building a network full of professionals with varying skillsets will certainly help you increase your knowledge, make better and more precise decisions, avoid mistakes and focus on expanding your business.

CHAPTER 10

Should I Start an LLC?

Should I start an LLC?

Should you form an LLC? If so, when? Do you do it before buying or after buying the property? A lot of newbie real estate investors think about this way more than necessary.

The first and most important piece of advice about LLCs is to not worry about them at all if you are starting new. You have a lot of work ahead you from searching for a property, analyzing it, securing financing and buying the property. Literally all of these steps have nothing to do with whether you form an LLC or not. So don't let the questions about the legal structure slow you down or prevent you from starting!

Generally, it is nearly impossible to secure financing in the name of an LLC. You will need a track record of regular income in the name of the company. And even then, it remains very difficult to get financing in the name of the company especially if you are just starting. You should expect that financing for the property will be in your name. What we will cover here are the pros and cons of transferring the deed of the property from your name to an LLC.

Before going any further, it is critical to recognize that the advice offered here is for informational purposes only. You should always seek professional advice from a legal or financial expert.

What is an LLC?

A Limited Liability Company (LLC) is a business structure and a legal form of a company that provides limited liability to its owner(s) in many jurisdictions.

Advantages of an LLC

Asset Liability Protection – Putting the property in an LLC offers asset liability protection. We live in a litigious society where people are unreasonably prone to go to law to settle disputes. In other words, a contractor or a tenant who woke up on the wrong side of the bed could sue you. If you are not protected sufficiently, your personal assets may be at risk. Putting the property in an LLC offers some protection so that if a tenant in that property decides to sue, your personal assets can be somewhat protected since the property is owned by the LLC and not directly by you. In the lawsuit, the LLC will be named as the defendant, not you. The assets owned by the LLC will be at risk, not yours.

Financial – There are several financial and tax advantages to forming an LLC. To name a few, you can easily open a checking account in the name of the LLC. This helps avoid commingling of funds. Also, you can easily and gradually transfer your ownership in the LLC to your heirs each year. On the long run, it becomes possible to pass the complete ownership of the assets owned by the LLC to your children or loves ones. This helps avoid deed recording and transfer fees.

Disadvantages of an LLC

Cost – Forming an LLC is not free. For example, in Virginia it costs $100 to form the LLC. In California, it costs $800. While this might not be a huge drawback, it is something to be considered and budgeted for. You will need to renew the LLC yearly. In Virginia, the renewal costs $50.

Due-On-Sale Clause – The mortgage agreement could contain a due-on-sale clause, this means that there is a chance of the lender calling the entire owed amount due immediately when you transfer the property to an LLC. Most investors agree that the chance of this happening is rare. So it is important to understand the risk.

To LLC or not to LLC

This is the question that you won't find a direct yes or no answer to anywhere. You need to look at your options and figure out if and when you may find it beneficial to transfer your property to an LLC.

Should you choose to proceed, one easy way to transfer the property to an LLC is simply reaching out to the title company you used for closing. They can quickly prepare a new deed for you. All you have to provide them with is the LLC documents showing the members and who can sign on behalf of the LLC. Then you need to sign it and have it notarized.

Finally, you send it back to the title company and they handle the rest.

Seeking professional advice is critical. The advice shared here should not be relied on alone without assistance from experts.

CHAPTER 11

Common Pitfalls

Common Pitfalls to Avoid

The world of real estate investing is a vast world full of complexities and intricacies. While your first real estate investment deal does not and should not have to be too complicated, it remains perhaps somewhat difficult and risky. Inherently, you can be prone to making mistakes simply because you are new to the subject and just starting out.

For that reason, it is imperative that you learn from other people's mistakes. Doing your homework and paying close attention to detail will help diminish the chance of failing in your first real estate deal.

"Learn from the mistakes of others. You can never live long enough to make them all yourself."
— Groucho Marx

Analysis paralysis

Analyzing and planning are very critical and necessary. But, overanalyzing excessively could prevent you from taking any action at all.

Analysis paralysis does not, in it of itself, lead you to making mistakes in real estate investing. Technically speaking, you cannot make a mistake if you don't even do anything. But think about it on the long run. Tomorrow, or 20 years down the road, will you look back and regret not investing in real estate? If the answer is yes, then analysis paralysis is your enemy today. Beat it! Take action.

Cynicism

Cynicism is a school of thought of ancient Greek philosophy. Cynics believe that the purpose of life is to live in virtue and in agreement with nature.

On the surface, cynicism is not necessarily bad. By the 19th century, emphasis on the negative aspects of cynicism led to the modern understanding of cynicism, which means a disposition of disbelief and skepticism in the sincerity of human motives and actions.

Cynics are skeptics. Excessive cynics take an overly defensive posture to protect themselves. This is particularly true with some of us who have been ripped off by someone in the past or stabbed in the back by a friend. Such experiences can make us even more cynical.

While being cynical can help us avoid getting manipulated by some, it can become toxic if we live our lives at all times by observing everything through the negative lens of skepticism. A healthy dose of cynicism is not bad. But always seeing the glass half empty can be detrimental to progress and change. Avoiding cynicism does not mean ignoring important facts.

When it comes to real estate investing, being an ultra cynic will lead you to inaction. You will spend your whole time focused on excuses for not investing in real estate. You will amplify negative thoughts and diminish anything positive you come across. You will think that the real estate agent is out there to get you. You will think that the banks are out there to rip you off. You will think that the property manager is hiding something. In a hot market, you will assume that it is completely impossible to find deals. In a down market, you will assume that the economy is ruined and investing in anything would be insane. In other words, a cynic is very much focused on identifying reasons for inaction.

Reject cynicism! Don't surround yourself with cynics who bring you down and draw you into their world of inaction.

Overconfidence

On the other hand, another pitfall to avoid is the overconfidence effect.

You meet a friend or two who tell you about their real estate experiences. You watch TV show where so-called experts discuss their forecasts for the market.

You read a book or two. Then, you jump into action and buy a real estate rental property that then sits vacant for months on end. This is the very definition of reckless confidence.

There is no exact science to balancing cynicism with confidence except common sense. Never assume that you know everything.

Learning is not a project that has an end date. It is a process that never ends, especially when it comes to complex economic and financial subjects like real estate investing.

Do your homework, get educated on the important basics of getting started in real estate investing, but proceed very cautiously.

Bad location

Who hasn't heard the mantra "location, location, location"? The word location is repeated three times for emphasis. Could this possibly be because location is so important important important?

Real estate properties, with the exception of mobile homes, cannot be moved. They are generally constructed with the idea of them remaining stationary in the same location. While this is excessively obvious, it is often underestimated.

Owners change, mortgages get refinanced, tenants come and go but the property remains in place in the same exact location. Selecting the right location to buy your first real estate investment property in is of paramount importance.

Defining what good or bad mean varies based on your tolerance for risk. But generally, it is very much recommended to limit your search to very good locations especially if you are new to real estate investing. Although there is money to be made in every market including undesired locations, your chance of failure increases exponentially.

Characteristics of good locations:

- Low crime rate
- High-rated schools
- Near amenities
- Near public transportation
- Near major employers

Characteristics of bad locations:
- Shady areas where crime is rampant
- Close to hazardous sites like landfills or toxic waste dumps
- Excessive noise from trains and flights
- Ghost towns with no jobs

There is no exact science to perfecting the location selection. This is especially true in evolving markets that may look undesirable today but are slowly but surely getting face-lifted and resurrected again. Think Detroit! It was a ghost town and many parts of it still are. But it is slowly changing with major employers moving in. There is no telling if the trend will continue. But this example goes to show that it is important, as always, to do your homework.

You can't possibly know everything. But you should know enough to avoid bad locations.

Emotions

Don't let emotions get involved in your decision-making. Analyzing the property based solely on cold facts is sufficient. Feeling excited and enthusiastic about investing in your first property is great but you should never allow your emotions to undermine the objective approach of adequate property analysis.

By allowing emotions to get in the way, we tend to be overly optimistic about the outcome. We tend to miscalculate the potential rental income by having high hopes of renting the property for more than the market value. If you love the property, you might make yourself believe that a tenant will see eye-to-eye with you and be willing to pay top dollars to rent it. This can be a fatal mistake that turns a good idea into a negative cash flow deal that you will regret.

Getting emotional about a property will lessen your ability to assess repair costs accurately. You tend to underestimate the level of effort involved in rehabbing the property.

Commingling funds

Simply put, it is best to maintain your business finances separately from your personal ones. If you have checking and savings bank accounts, don't deposit the rental income in them. Don't cut checks to contractors from them.

Instead, it is best to set up separate bank accounts for your real estate business needs. Whether you do this under the name of an LLC or not is unrelated. The fact remains that it is significantly easier and clearer to maintain all real estate related transactions in separate bank accounts.

For example, if you are driving to a new location to scope out the area and see several properties that you might invest in, you can use the debit card or credit card of your business for expenses incurred during the trip such as filling up gas or paying for parking at the location.

1031 Exchange

In a nutshell, a 1031 Exchange is a swap of one asset for another. Most swaps of assets are taxable but a 1031 Exchange can be tax free.

Generally speaking, when you sell an asset, you have to pay taxes on the gains. If you sell an investment property, pocket the profit and dump it in your savings account, you will have to pay taxes on any gains. This is obviously a mistake if you intend on buying another property shortly thereafter.

In a 1031 Exchange, you can avoid paying taxes on the gains if you swap the real estate property you just sold for another like-kind one within the designated timeframe specified by the IRS as long as you never have direct access to the cash gained from the sale. The IRS specifies that you must designate a replacement property within 45 days and close within 6 months. You should not receive any cash at all, otherwise, it is taxed.

To perform a 1031 Exchange properly, you need to insert a special clause in the purchase and sale agreement specifying that you are relinquishing the property and will be exchanging it for another one. The funds received from the sale of the property should not go to you but rather to a qualified intermediary of your choosing such as a bank or law firm. The intermediary will handle the funds throughout the 1031 Exchange transaction. You should never have direct control over the funds. You should identify one or several replacement properties and communicate that in writing to the intermediary within 45 days and then close on the property within 6 months of the sale of the relinquished property or the due date of that year's income-tax return, whichever comes first. Finally, you need to file IRS form 8824 with the IRS to effectively defer the taxes.

There is no limit to the number of times you can do a 1031 Exchange. You can keep repeating the process as long as you want from one property to another while avoiding paying capital gains.

As always, it is highly recommended to seek professional help from an attorney, tax specialist or accountant since 1031 Exchanges can be very tricky given the strict IRS requirements at a federal level and potential additional state level requirements.

Insurance protection

Lack of adequate insurance protection can be a common pitfall in the world of real estate investing. As with everything, this also varies based on your tolerance for risk.

In addition to general property insurance and liability insurance on the rental property, it is a good idea to also have a personal umbrella insurance policy.

A Personal Catastrophe Liability (PLC) coverage (personal umbrella insurance), can give you an extra layer of protection. For a nominal fee usually around

$200 a year, you can get $1 million in additional coverage for covered claims brought against you or your family for things like bodily injury and accidental damage to another person's property. A PCL policy typically kicks in when other insurance coverage is exhausted.

CHAPTER 12

Controversial American Dream

What is the American Dream?

According to Merriam-Webster, the American Dream is:

"a happy way of living that is thought of by many Americans as something that can be achieved by anyone in the U.S. especially by working hard and becoming successful with good jobs, a nice house, two children, and plenty of money..."

Yes of course, it is indeed true that the U.S. is the land of opportunity in so many ways. But, is buying a house for you and your family to live in so important to achieving and enjoying the American dream?

Home Ownership

Home ownership is the quintessential goal of many Americans. It represents the most perfect example of quality or class. Arguably, homeownership builds wealth. Many Americans work hard, save money and put down a down payment to buy a personal residence. The hope is that the house will increase in value. Over time, the homeowner will have more equity in the house. This is achieved with the potential increase in property value and the slow reduction of principal (amount owed) by simply paying the monthly mortgage payments.

But is your own house an investment?

It is often said that buying your own house is the single most important investment in your life. This assumption is flawed for many reasons. The premise of potential increase in value is not alone a good reason to assume that buying a personal residence is a good investment.

Don't be disappointed. The house you live in is not an investment!

Yes, real estate values have the potential of appreciating dramatically. But when was this ever guaranteed? Although likely, there is no guarantee that the value will increase! And even if it does, it might not increase enough to outpace inflation and offset the carrying costs and expenses of owning and living in the house.

For the house to be an investment, it must be treated as an investment. You must have complete control over it as a business. This is often very difficult to accomplish in a personal residence because you live in it. Your family lives in it. Your kids go to the schools in the neighborhood. Packing up and moving is far from convenient. The fact that the house increased in value does not really matter if you don't have access to the cash. For it to be an investment, you must maintain control over the ability to sell and cash out the equity, and use that equity to make more money. Even those who sell and cash out the equity often end up upgrading and moving to a more expensive house and then repeat the process again and again and again. This could increase wealth but only in one single property that is a money pit left right and center.

And even if you borrow money on the house by leveraging a home equity line of credit (HELOC) or by refinancing, it still does not matter. None of these strategies change the fact that your house is still not an investment. It doesn't change the fact that the bulk of your hard-earned money is still trapped in the house. The HELOC is also more debt acquired that you have to pay off with interest. What if the house drops in value and you end up underwater owing on it more than its market value? Refinancing is also overrated because it does again reset the amortization table and puts you in a position paying a ton of interest while pushing the payoff date of the mortgage to another 15 or 30 years down the road. This is the definition of insanity!

The house you live in is nothing but a glorified savings account, at best!

Your own house is a liability

If you live in the house, then it is not an investment. Instead, it is a liability.

This is controversial and not everyone agrees. But think about it. If the house is costing you money and not making you any money, then how can it possibly be an investment? Let's set the terminology aside. Suppose you insist on labeling your own house as an "investment", how can it possibly be a good investment? How can it possibly be the best place to invest your money when you can achieve higher rates of return on your money by buying rental properties?

Owning a house costs money, lots of money. The bigger and more expensive the house is, the more money it will cost you on the long run. All that is just to live in it! All the house is providing you with is shelter.

Not only do you have to set aside a large down payment to buy the property, but you also have to make the mortgage payments, pay real estate taxes, insurance, utilities, repairs and maintenance. You can't forget to account for the expenses of costly repairs that will most definitely be needed over the long run. Sooner or later, you will need to replace the roof, heater, HVAC system, windows, flooring and appliances. How about that bathroom or kitchen remodel you've been thinking about? Add all these up and you're looking at tens of thousands of dollars.

It's easy to justify these costs because, after all, you live in the house. No one is disputing the necessity of these expenses. No one is suggesting ignoring a leaky roof and settling for a water bucket. The house provides shelter. It needs to be safe and comfortable. But this gets back to the main point that the house you live in is not an investment. It costs you money and doesn't make you money; therefore, it is a liability.

Let's talk numbers

Wait, there is more! It is bad as it is that the house you live in costs a lot of money to upkeep. But it gets worse. Let's hammer the main point again that your primary residence does not generate any cash flow.

It is very important to distinguish between your primary residence and an investment rental property. When you invest in a rental property, you expect it to make you money. You expect monthly cash flow from the property in the form of rental income. This is the cash flow that is completely non-existent in your primary residence. Why in the world would you dedicate most of your energy towards an asset that does not generate income?

Your own residence

For example, you buy a house for you and your family to live in for $200,000. The specifics of financing don't really matter. But the point is that you will be sinking $200,000 plus interest of your own hard-earned money in one single address over the long run.

Suppose you put $40,000 down and finance the remaining $160,000 at 4% for 30 years. You would be looking at a total of $114,991 in interest and $96,000 in taxes and insurance over 30 years. This assumes that you stay put in the same place and don't refinance. If you move and upgrade to a bigger and more expensive house, the situation deteriorates exponentially especially when it comes to the debt cost. Every time you start back at the top of the amortization table, you start to pay much more interest and less principal again. It's a never-ending vicious cycle.

Continuing with the same assumptions, now we're looking at the total of all payments being $410,991 over 30 years.

We arrive at this number by adding:

- $40,000 down payment
- $160,000 principal
- $114,991 interest
- $96,000 taxes and insurance

Wait, there is more! Let's assume that you replace the roof, HVAC, heater, a few windows, and appliances. We all know that appliances are not going to last more than 10 to 15 years. So we will assume that they all will be replaced just once for the sake of not making this example overly aggressive. And, do you think you will settle with that old kitchen or bathroom for 15 or 30 years? It's unlikely. Let's factor in only $15,000 for remodeling budget, which is extremely conservative.

When it's all said and done, you will be looking at a minimum of $42,000.

At this rate, the total cost of owning and carrying the costs of your own house will certainly exceed $453,000. All this is just for a primary residence that is making you no money at all. Even if the property increased in value, it doesn't matter because all that money is still trapped in the property. You have to borrow money on the property, refinance or sell it to have access to that cash. And plus, the appreciation is not even guaranteed to keep up with inflation in the first place.

The market could crash. The economy could tank. A lifelong worth of hard work could remain trapped in one single address.

Investment Properties

Going back to the property analysis chapter, we learned that investing $24,000 to buy a $120,000 rental property could yield $7,140 in annual cash flow. Think of the magnitude of the strategy differences between arguably wasting $410,991 of your own money on your personal residence compared to investing at least part of that money over time in rental properties.

If you manage to buy four properties, you will be cash flowing $28,560 yearly while the rental income from the tenants is effectively paying down the mortgages on the properties for you over time. You will be running a business and increasing wealth exponentially compared to having all your money stuck in one personal house with no other sources of income.

You can set aside the income earned and use it to buy even more properties. But let's assume that you stop at just four properties. Stretch that income over 30 years, and you will be looking at a minimum of $856,800 in cash earned from just those four rentals.

This doesn't even take into consideration increases in rental income or the priceless fact that the properties will be completely paid off in 30 years as well. This is a total of $480,000 in equity.

So what

So what are we really suggesting here? Are we saying that buying a personal residence is a big mistake? Not always! Are we saying that renting is the smart way to go? Maybe! The answer is very difficult and varies drastically based on the area you live in, your family needs, your investment strategy and your financial goals.

If you are working hard 9 to 5 just to spend your money on mortgage payments and car loan/lease payments, then you are wasting your energy! It is certainly wiser to dedicate your financial energy towards assets that make you money such as investment rental properties that produce monthly cash flow. This strategy could lead one day to financial independence.

You could get to the point where the rental income exceeds your job's salary. You could even buy more properties and use the income to cover the rental costs of the house or apartment you are renting. You could then revise your plan and decide to buy your own house. But at this point, you have assets producing income that can help make the mortgage payments of your own house.

Now you are no longer fully dependent on your job's income! You can finally hop off the hamster wheel! You are financially independent.

The general piece of advice here is to avoid dedicating large chunks of your hard-earned money to your personal residence whether it's owned or rented.

Renting certainly gives you the advantage of mobility. It's easier to move without having to worry about timing the sale when the market is hot. You won't have to worry about repairs, maintenance or remodeling when living in a rental. You can simply choose another more modern rental to move to. You can do this while investing in several rental properties.

What's wrong with living in a rented house or apartment while working on owning and renting several other properties?

You can build wealth by owning rental properties. You don't have to buy your own!

There is one exception to be noted. If you buy a duplex or a large enough house that you could rent half of it, then the case can be made that the house is an investment, at least partially. But other than this, it remains important to acknowledge the facts and accept the reality that your primary residence is not an investment.

The American dream should be about seizing opportunities where found. It should be about doing well and achieving wealth. It does not have to involve buying a house to live in.

Buying a house to live in and upgrading three times in a lifetime is the American dream of American banks.

It should not be yours.

CHAPTER 13

Final Words

So you've finished reading this guide. Awesome! You have just accomplished a big first step in your real estate investment journey. But despite learning more by finishing this guide, this is no time to rest on your laurels. You have not done anything yet!

Now it is completely and utterly up to you, and no one by you, where you take it from here.

How successful you become is all up to you

The great thing about investing is that success depends largely on the actions you take. There is no employer or boss to have to deal with. You are in total control of how successful you become. If you shelf this guide and do nothing with the information learned, you won't achieve anything. If you decide to learn more and take action, you would be surprised by what you could accomplish.

Action yields results! Inaction, well, is just that!

Don't aim for perfection

If you overanalyze everything and stress about being perfect, you will remain stuck in analysis paralysis. Move on to the next step. Talk to people. Build a team, connect and network with professionals and other investors who share similar interests. Take small baby steps and then tweak your plans and strategies as you go along.

Be patient

Results don't come overnight. You can't expect to achieve complete financial independence by investing in one property. You can't expect to buy 20 rental properties in 6 months either. There are limits to how fast you can accomplish your goals. Take your time. Be patient!

Don't give up

Most people who give up often do so when they are very close to achieving their objectives. Don't let anything stop you from achieving your goals. Never forget that you are not the only one attempting this. Others have invested in real estate successfully and still do so everyday. There is no reason that you cannot do the same.

Ask for help. Persevere. Never give up!

Best for luck!

CHAPTER 14

Bonus Content

Most Important Content

Bonus Template – Rental Property Analysis

This worksheet is the most important piece of the puzzle for your property analysis needs. At least for me, I rely on this template very heavily. All you need to do is input data in the cells highlighted in green. All the rest is automatically calculated. It's important to get familiar with the formulas. Go ahead and click on them to see how the calculations work. And reference the property analysis chapter to learn more and connect the dots.

Bonus Template – Mortgage Amortization with Extra Payments

This worksheet makes is super easy to calculate dynamically the amortization table while showing the impact of making additional monthly payments towards the principal. Modify the data in the green cells. The rest is automatically calculated.

Less Important Content

Complete guide of lead automation

Does the sheer number of properties on the market overwhelm you? Are you having a hard time keeping track of the properties you are analyzing? Automating the process using online systems is the way to go. The step-by-step guide with screenshot on how to create a system to manage your property analysis will solve this problem for you.

Maximum conforming loan limits per county

(FullCountyLoanLimitList2017_HERA-BASED_FINAL_FLAT.xlsx)

Fannie Mae and Freddie Mac Maximum Loan Limits for Mortgages Acquired in Calendar Year 2017 and Originated after 10/1/2011 or before 7/1/2007.

These limits were determined under the provisions of the Housing and Economic Recovery Act of 2008.

Savings accounts annual average interest rate

This goes to show that interest rates on traditional Savings accounts are very low. Therefore, investing your money and making your money work for you is important.

Other Free Bonus Material

We will send you free bonus material in the future when they become available. Any new useful worksheet or helpful features we come up with will be shared with you automatically.

Get your bonus content

To receive your bonus content, visit the page below or scan the QR code:

http://curiousroy.com/real-estate-books/

Disclaimer

It is recommended that you work with a qualified professional in all aspects of real estate investing. This ensures you will receive the most favorable tax treatment and also help you avoid any surprises at tax time.

The ideas and strategies outlined in this guide should never be used without first assessing your own personal and financial situation, or without consulting a financial professional.

The information contained herein is not intended to be a source of financial or real estate advice with respect to the material presented, and the information and/or documents contained in this guide do not constitute investment advice.

The content in this guide is intended to be used and must be used for informational purposes only. I am not a financial professional. By reading the content you assume complete responsibility for any actions you take as a result.

www.ingramcontent.com/pod-product-compliance
Lightning Source LLC
Chambersburg PA
CBHW020434220526
45464CB00002B/705